How to LIVE LIFE & LOVE IT

by Rex Humbard

Rex Humbard Ministry
Box 3063
Boca Raton, Florida 33431

HOW TO LIVE LIFE
AND LOVE IT

When I think of the many friends and partners our ministry has, I am overwhelmed. When I look at the many people who have given so much of themselves to help me take the gospel to lost souls all over the world, it makes me realize how fortunate I am. It helps me focus on the blessings of God, rather than the burdens of this huge worldwide television ministry.

Of course, the burden is still there. It has always been part of the picture, because the load of this ministry is great. The call of God to this worldwide mission takes a huge toll on the bodies, minds, and the budgets of the people who have pledged their lives to it. A worldwide television ministry requires colossal commitment on the part of the leadership, the staff, the partners, and everyone connected with it.

So it is easy to focus attention on that burden and

spend all our time working to lift it, to lighten the physical, spiritual, and financial load from our shoulders.

It is a worthwhile goal, sure. Sharing the burden of this worldwide ministry is part of fulfilling Christ's Great Commission, "Go ye into all the world, and preach the gospel to every creature" (Mark 16:15).

Everyone who joins us in this great task is accepting Christ's direction and obeying the Word of God. And, in giving of yourself to this ministry, you are sure to be blessed for your obedience to that Great Commission of Christ.

But as I seek the Lord's leading in writing this book, He is prompting me in another area.

Instead of seeking your help for the great needs of this ministry, I want to help *you* as you struggle with *your* needs. Instead of asking to *get* help, I am writing this book to *give* help.

In this way, I am obeying God's law of giving and receiving, His principle of seedtime and harvest: "Give, and it shall be given unto you; good measure, pressed down, and shaken together, and running over (Luke 6:38).

As I give to you, as I help you with solutions to the problems in your life, I am trusting in God's promise — trusting that my needs, and the needs of our television ministry, will be met. As I minister to you, I believe God will use you to minister to me, and will use you to meet the needs of our television ministry around the world.

6

As I write these words, I am praying for you.

I am praying that God will open your heart to these spiritual truths.

I am praying that you will open your life to the leading of the Holy Spirit, and that you will allow yourself to be used of God in His kingdom.

And I am praying that through obedience to the Word of God you will learn to live life and love it — as never before.

The worldwide television ministry fills my heart with excitement. I want to share with you the beautiful blessings God is pouring out on us as we reach lost souls around the world. I want to share the needs of the ministry with you. I want you to let God bless you by becoming a member of our Prayer Key Family and a partner in fulfilling the Great Commission of Christ through our ministry together "to all the world."

But this book is set aside.

It is for you. It is written to help you solve your personal problems. It is given to you as a gift of love, to help you become a happier, healthier, more fulfilled person.

It is a book for single adults, to help you live your life and love it.

It is a book for husbands and wives, designed to help you achieve a deeper love for one another in the coming months.

It is a book for fathers and mothers, designed to help you live life with your children and love it.

It is a book for young people, especially for teenagers, to help you actually enjoy your parents and what they represent. It will help you build a foundation right now for a great life in the future.

It is a book for Grandma and Grandpa, mother-in-law and father-in-law, to help you fulfill your delicate roles appropriately and happily.

It is a book for senior citizens, designed to help *you* enjoy your life as never before.

It is a book for church members, deacons, stay-at-homes, and even preachers.

A book designed to help you live life and love it as never before.

This book is written to help you unlock the windows of heaven, to help you receive from God the blessings He has provided for those who know and love Him.

This is a textbook, but also a workbook. It is a "how-to" book, a practical guide for harvesting happiness through three principles of obedience: to man's laws, nature's laws, and God's laws.

And it is my prayer for you, friend, that you will be blessed in a new and unusual way as you read it.

Rex Humbard

TABLE OF CONTENTS

1

HOW TO BREAK
THE LAW

A man was running down a sidewalk in the rain. He was going to be late for work. He came to the corner and started running across the wet street against the traffic light.

A policeman saw him and shouted "Stop!" because the man was challenging the law that says, "Pedestrians cross only on green."

As he hurried on down the sidewalk on the other side of the street, he slipped on the wet pavement and lost his balance and fell. He knocked himself unconscious because he challenged the law that says, "The human skull can't take much of a pounding."

The man never woke up. He died in the hospital and his soul slipped into eternity. There the man was cast into eternal darkness, because he had not given heed to the law that Jesus spoke: "No man cometh unto the Father, but by me" (John 14:6).

Your life is wrapped around three different kinds of laws: man's laws, nature's laws, and God's laws.

The Bible talks about all three in a single verse of Scripture — III John:2, which says:

"Beloved, I wish above all things that thou mayest prosper and be in health, even as thy soul prospereth."

"I would that ye prosper (referring to man's laws), and be in health (referring to nature's laws), even as thy soul prospers (referring to God's laws)."

Mankind has created a complicated arrangement of rules and regulations by which we are to live our lives. Almost everything we do, minute by minute and hour by hour, is regulated by one man-made law or another.

Traffic flows through our cities according to man-made laws. We make a living through trade, which is regulated by man-made interest rates, minimum wages, and commercial regulations.

We pay taxes according to man's law. We elect leaders according to man's law. We even set our clocks and wristwatches according to man-made time zones.

Nature has its own laws, and they can be rigid. Gravity is a law of nature that refuses to be broken. Only with great skill have we been able to suspend this natural law to get airplanes and rockets into the air. Still, almost everything eventually winds back down to earth.

Nature's law includes the weather, a thing both unpredictable and barely manageable. Scientists can now sometimes force clouds to rain, but they have yet to create a cloud from scratch. We are still at the mercy of the weather every day of our lives. Nature's laws require us to dress warmly in the winter and slow down on wet pavement, to stay away from people with contagious diseases, and to get some sleep once in a while.

God has laws too.

All of God's laws are spelled out in the Bible, which is His Word for mankind. He requires us to love one another as we love ourselves (Matthew 19:19). He commands us to go into all the world and preach the gospel to every creature (Mark 16:15), a law that I have tried to obey personally through our worldwide television ministry. He tells us to accept Christ, His Son, as our personal Saviour if we hope to see the heavenly Father in eternity (John 14:6). The Ten Commandments are a good example of God's laws (Exodus 20:1-17).

You may think of laws as life-wreckers, but laws are actually live-savers.

Laws are blessings. They are designed to bless. Laws make life easier and more comfortable, or more fulfilling in some way.

You may growl at that long red light, but man's traffic laws keep your old jalopy moving along as speedily and safely as possible through the local traffic.

You may wish you could jog 20 miles a day, but the pain in your chest reminds you about nature's laws.

This is nature's way of keeping you from killing yourself.

God's laws work the same way. They, more than any others, are designed to bless you.

"Know ye that the Lord he is God: it is he that hath made us, and not we ourselves; we are his people, and the sheep of his pasture" (Psalm 100:3).

God created you Himself. He loves you, and He wants more than anything else for you to be blessed.

So He established His laws to do just that. And, as long as you obey God's laws, He blesses you.

The problem we human beings keep running into is our universal urge to break the law.

We want to do it our way. We want to be in charge, running the show. We want to be calling the shots.

Even the apostle Paul struggled with this urge: "For I know that in me (that is, in my flesh,) dwelleth no good thing . . . O wretched man that I am!" (Romans 7:18,24).

We want to be the lawmakers. And that usually turns us into lawbreakers.

So we push the speed limit a little bit, challenging man's laws. So we stay up a little too late or drink a little liquor at a party, challenging natural laws. So we share a little nasty gossip about that lady up the street who rubs us the wrong way, and we challenge God's laws.

It may not seem too big a crime at the moment. It probably looks very small . . . something nobody will ever notice, something you will never get caught for.

But every law, when it is broken, changes from a blessing to a burden.

I saw this so clearly when I went to Brazil last year with my family and our television crew, to hold televised crusade meetings in the huge soccer stadiums of the major cities in that nation.

On the way down to Brazil, our photographer Helmut Jilling realized he had forgotten his passport. To travel from the United States to Brazil, an American citizen is required to have a passport. This is one of man's laws. It is a law designed to help the American citizen. It gives him the protection of his own federal government as he travels in a foreign country.

But Helmut was already on the airplane; and he had forgotten the passport, thousands of miles behind us. As our flight was landing in Brazil, Helmut was nervous, like a driver doing 50 miles per hour in a 35-miles-per-hour zone and keeping his eyes open for police cars. (Even a person who doesn't get caught must bear the burden of breaking the law!)

All the rest of our crew made it through customs, except Helmut. Without his passport, he was not allowed to enter the country. We all laughed about it later, but as the customs officials placed the frightened photographer under arrest, we were all extremely frightened. The rest of us had to leave Helmut behind as we flew on to the next city.

For five full days Helmut was kept in official custody, unable to leave his quarters, until finally his passport arrived from the United States. It cost Helmut a huge amount of money to get his passport shipped in, and before his release he had to pay a fine of several hundred dollars. He had broken a law. He had to pay the price, in lost time and money, as well as the playful teasing of his friends among our staff.

The law, which was designed to protect Helmut when he traveled overseas, had become a burden instead of a blessing . . . all because he had broken man's law.

Every law, once broken, turns from a blessing into a burden.

My wife Maude Aimee found this principle to be true of *natural* laws, too.

She was also in Brazil with our family at that time, ministering in the great rallies all across that huge country. She was working night and day, even after the doctor had told her that her body was too weak for such exertion.

"You've got to slow down," he told her firmly.

But Maude Aimee was too excited about the impact of our ministry in South America. She was too dedicated to stop and take it easy. She kept right on singing and speaking and traveling with us from city to city — until finally, one day, her natural body broke down. Her heart was suddenly blocked, and she had to be rushed to a Brazilian hospital.

Maude Aimee's speaking and singing and traveling suddenly ended. She was completely silenced as her body demanded she pay the penalty for breaking nature's laws.

Nature's law had required a little rest and relaxation along the way, but Maude Aimee hadn't obeyed that law.

For months my own family and I waited so anxiously for her to recuperate. It was a long, slow process. She was desperately sick day after day. The healing was unsteady, touch-and-go, as Maude Aimee had to learn to obey nature's laws and take care of her natural body.

Even though many friends were praying for her, all over the world, Maude Aimee had to pay the price for breaking nature's law of rest and relaxation. It was designed to bless; but now that it was broken, it had become a tremendous burden.

Remember, a law once broken turns from blessing into burden.

And this principle is also true of God's laws.

God's preference is that we be blessed. "I wish above all things that thou mayest prosper," the Bible says in III John:2, "and be in health, even as thy soul prospereth." But if we break God's laws, we must pay the price. The breaking of God's law is called *sin*. And, "the wages of sin," the Bible tells us, "is death" (Romans 6:23), or loss of fellowship with God.

Broken laws give you most of your problems in life.

The Bible declares that "every transgression and disobedience" receives "a just recompense of reward" (Hebrews 2:2).

Most of your burdens were originally designed to

be blessings. But someone has broken some law and turned that blessing into a burden. Usually the lawbreaker causing *me* the most problems is the one I see in the mirror when I comb my hair.

So, if you have a problem in your life, it's best to begin solving it yourself. God's Word says, "let us cleanse ourselves from all filthiness of the flesh and spirit" (II Corinthians 7:1). This is *your* job, because God's law says so.

Are you obeying all of man's laws? Are you challenging any of nature's laws? Are you in tune with God's laws? Are you living a Christ-centered life, loving God with all your heart, and loving others as much as you love yourself?

Answer these questions honestly, and you'll find the root of most of your problems in life. And you've already taken the first step toward living life and loving it.

But it doesn't stop there . . .

2

THE DIRT-COVERED CHILD

We don't simply look at our problems, find out why they're happening, and then spend our whole lives suffering with them.

You have a helper.

A short time ago I received a 12-page typewritten letter from a lady whose life seemed completely hopeless. I can't even remember how many times she had been married and divorced, and she had a host of emotional and spiritual problems besides.

In the natural, there was no hope for her life ever to be better.

There seemed to be no chance of her learning to live

life and love it ever again. How could even God bring her out of this mess? How could she ever know peace in her heart?

I had no answer.

But I prayed for that lady anyway, because she had acted in faith by writing to me and sharing her needs.

Soon I got a second letter from the lady. No, her circumstances were no different. There had been no supernatural miracle of God to change her life-situation.

But God had answered prayer. He had moved in her heart. He had changed her perspectives, her attitudes.

"I have learned," she wrote in that second letter, "that God can build my life from right where I am. I don't have to get good for Him first — He will lead me there Himself!"

You have someone who loves you and cares about you and is *involved* in your life.

That helper is God. God loves you, He cares about you. He is also committed to you.

Remember God is not against you for your sins, He is for you against your sins.

"There is therefore now no condemnation to them which are in Christ Jesus . . . who are the called according to his purpose" (Romans 8:1,28).

God doesn't love you less if you have problems. Even the most outstanding Christians have struggles. "For all have sinned," the Bible says, "and come short of the glory of God" (Romans 3:23). God loves you where you are, whatever your condition may be.

Do you love your child any less when he comes home covered with dirt? No. Neither does God love you any less when you come to Him covered with sin.

All you have to do is ask Him to forgive you and He will cleanse you and clean you up. He does it gladly, because His Son Jesus Christ already paid the penalty for your sins, when He died for you on Calvary's cross.

Since your debt is already paid, God is anxious for you to accept your freedom. You don't have to spend your whole life in the prison of your sins. God loves you and wants to set you free by the power of His Son Jesus.

Accepting Christ as your personal Saviour in this way is the first step toward overcoming your problems, the first step toward getting in harmony with God's laws, the first step toward learning how to live life and love it.

And it doesn't require any special ceremony or ritual. If you want to accept Christ as your personal Saviour right now, just pray this simple little prayer to the heavenly Father and mean it sincerely in your heart as you pray:

"Father, I am sorry for my sins. I come to you dirty, but I ask you to make me clean. Thank you for letting your Son Jesus pay the debt for my sins. Right now I accept your forgiveness through the sacrifice that Jesus made for me. I love you, Father, and I will live my life for you. Thank you, Father. Amen."

When you ask Christ into your life He forgives your sins immediately. Your past is forgotten by Him. He gives you a fresh start.

Still every human being seems to break a variety of God's laws every day. You can always go to your heavenly Father and ask Him to forgive you for these broken laws, because the Bible says,

"If we confess our sins, he is faithful and just to forgive us our sins, and to cleanse us from all unrighteousness" (I John 1:9).

As you study God's Word you will draw closer to God and you will learn more and more how to live in the light of God's love, how to stay in harmony with God's laws.

And remember, God loves you where you are.

"Who shall separate us from the love of Christ?" the Bible asks in Romans 8:35.

A young man once got angry with his wife and murdered her, then tried to escape the penalty of man's laws. He sneaked from one state to the next, until finally the law caught up with him and put him in prison to serve a life sentence.

I prayed with this young man months later, in prison, and he accepted Christ, asking God to forgive his sins. Then the boy's mother began telling him that God was going to get him released from prison because Jesus had paid his debts.

When I heard the young man excitedly explaining all of this, I had to tell him otherwise.

If you have a mortgage on your house when you accept Christ, God doesn't suddenly pay off that mortgage for you. You still owe it to man, according to man's laws.

"Jesus loves you where you are," I told him. "He's paid your penalty before God, but you still have to pay the penalty for breaking the laws of man. Jesus told us to 'render unto Caesar that which is Caesar's' (Matthew 22:21) — to obey the laws of man. You owe the State of Pennsylvania a debt for breaking its laws. You will have to pay with the years of your life. That doesn't mean God doesn't love you, but *every debt must be paid.*"

You may have heard me talk about the principle of seedtime and harvest, and God's law of giving and receiving. It's a beautiful principle of life which God ordained. "Give, and it shall be given unto you" (Luke 6:38). It is true in every area of life: If you give of your time, your talent, your love, your finances, God always gives back to you.

But the law of giving and receiving works all the time, whether you are living inside or outside the law.

"Be not deceived;" the Bible reminds us, "God is not mocked: for whatsoever a man soweth, that shall he also reap" (Galatians 6:7).

This is the principle of seedtime and harvest stated another way. However you state it, and however you use it, it is still absolutely the truth in every case.

You reap what you sow.

This is how God established the world, on the principle that you get back whatever you put in. If you sow evil seeds, you reap evil fruit. If you plant righteousness, you harvest righteousness. If you set out to hurt that nasty neighbor of yours, you're going to get hurt yourself. When you decide to love that nasty neighbor, you are bound to receive abundant love in return.

That's why every broken law demands a price.

In fact, you never break the law. The law always breaks you. The debt is always paid.

The Bible even says in many cases our debts must be paid by our children and grandchildren or by our friends and loved ones. "I the Lord thy God am . . . visiting the iniquity of the fathers upon the children unto the third and fourth generation" (Exodus 20:5).

How many divorcees come from divorce-torn

homes? Every species produces "after his (own) kind" (Genesis 1:12,24). Every sin is a broken law, and every broken law requires the payment of a penalty.

When I was still a teenager I heard this principle illustrated in an ugly and tragic way.

I joined the band in high school, and we often traveled to neighboring communities to play for football games, parades, and concerts. Every trip was a big chance for most fellows in the band to drink, smoke, and live it up. They scoffed at me because I wouldn't join them, but I refused anyway. Even as a teenager, I could see they were grossly defying the laws of God.

Then one day our band director had taken as much of this kind of conduct as he could stand. He sat us boys down and told us a story about two friends of his.

These two friends were in college, walking home from a late class one night. They had to walk through a part of town where prostitutes lined the streets and called out invitations to them.

It had happened before — every time they walked home — but the two friends had never stopped. Finally, however, one night, one of the friends turned off the street and went in.

The other friend walked on home alone.

Years passed. The two friends hadn't seen each other for a long time — when they finally ran into each other one day.

One of the friends invited the other to his home. There, he took his visitor to the back yard. The yard

25

was surrounded by a high wooden fence, shielding it from the view of any neighbors.

Chained to the fence was a stout little boy who looked like an animal. He was living like a wild dog, with his hair matted, his skin filthy, his clothes ragged. He had almost no mentality, and every so often he went flying into a mad rage. In between the fits, his eyes glazed over as if he were drugged.

"Do you remember that night I stopped at the prostitute's place?" the owner of the home asked his friend. "That night I contracted a terrible disease. This is my son. He inherited my disease the moment he was born. He is paying the penalty for what I did as a teenager. You reap what you sow."

Friend, you cannot just use Jesus like a fire alarm, begging miracles when you have a penalty to pay. Christ will pay your debt to God. Still, every debt must be paid by someone.

Of course God can work miracles. He could have released that young man from the Pennsylvania State Prison. He could have healed that man's terribly diseased son. God's power is greater than any in the universe.

But God expects us to walk in daily obedience to man's laws and nature's laws as well as His own. We must maintain a balance between the three.

I'm a Christian, and I'm a preacher; but I'll be in trouble if I disobey nature's laws — regardless of my spirituality. I may say, "I'm going to fast and pray all day and all night." That's fine. That's obedience to God's law.

But then, if I go out and lie down in knee-deep snow during my prayer and fasting, I'm violating nature's law. Nature's law says my natural body is going to freeze to death — even though I'm obeying God's law at the very same time!

Don't blame God for your suffering when you've defiled your body by violating nature's laws — God didn't put that suffering on you. You did it.

We must achieve a harmony between man's laws, nature's laws, and God's laws.

But remember, even as you keep these principles of obedience in your life, you will still have some problems to face. And even so, God loves you. Just because you have problems doesn't mean God doesn't love you.

He loves you through your problems. He loves you regardless of your struggles. In fact, God can *use* your problems to teach you how to live more like Jesus Christ. And that, after all, is the most victorious life known to man!

Just how God uses your problems as teaching tools is the subject of our next chapter.

3

EVERY PROBLEM HAS A PURPOSE

So you've made a mistake, you've broken man's law, or nature's law, or God's law . . . and now you're paying the price. You're facing some kind of struggle in your life.

God cares about you and loves you. It may not be obvious to you now, while you're suffering. But even while you are paying that debt, God is using that problem as a teaching tool. He is turning that burden back into a blessing. He is turning that disadvantage back into an advantage. And if you learn His lesson in your problem, you will come out of your problem a better Christian and a happier person!

Every problem you face has a purpose. If God doesn't solve your problem directly with a miracle, it must mean that He has a *reason* for letting you face your problem.

When God allows problems to enter your life, He does it to *teach* you the Christ-walk.

Every problem is a healthy challenge to the believer. By allowing that problem into my life, God is challenging me to *grow* in Him.

Of course the challenge of a problem can have two very different results. I can either *accept* the challenge and *grow* through my problem . . .

. . . Or, I can *fail* to meet the challenge, and then I will be *defeated* by my problem.

When you face problems in your life, ask yourself, "What law have I broken — man's law — nature's law — God's law — that I may be paying for?

Then ask the Lord to teach you and lead you by His Holy Spirit as you accept the challenge and face that problem.

This is the believer's hope — faith in God! "Now faith is the substance of things hoped for, the evidence of things not seen" (Hebrews 11:1).

If you have faith in God as your loving heavenly Father, you can have faith that He will not allow your problems to crush you.

God has a great investment in you. He created you, and He wants you to fellowship with Him.

So He is not going to let you slip down the drain. He will not leave you helpless.

You can also have faith in God to teach you whatever it is He wants you to learn from your problems. You can have faith that God will not just waste your energy, your mind, your health, on problems without some divine purpose.

God has a plan for you, and learning through your problems is part of that plan.

The Bible calls believers "joint-heirs with Christ," and says, "if so be that we suffer with him, that we may be also glorified together" (Romans 8:17).

Problems are a common experience. Everyone has them. God can use your problems to help you in your Christian life, if you will just open your heart to His teaching.

Think of your problems as the pages of a textbook. They may not be fun to wade through, but they are full of valuable information. And by the time you get to the last one, it will be time to graduate!

Heaven is our goal. It is the finish line at the end of this earthly obstacle course. Our problems are only temporary. They will disappear in a few days, a few years, and we will be home with our Father.

The apostle Paul kept this in mind even while he was facing the problem of imprisonment — a problem more terrible than most of us have ever faced!

"For I reckon," he wrote to the Roman Christians, "that the sufferings of this present time are not worthy to be compared with the glory which shall be revealed in us" (Romans 8:18).

"For our light affliction," he also wrote to the believers at Corinth, "which is but for a moment, worketh for us a far more exceeding and eternal weight of glory" (II Corinthians 4:17).

Paul kept heaven on his mind.

"We look not at the things which are seen," he wrote in the next verse to the Corinthians, "but at the things which are not seen: for the things which are seen are temporal; but the things which are not seen are eternal."

Think of the apostle Paul. We usually see him as a great success, a marvelous example of a Christian. And he was.

But by the standards of today's world Paul was a failure! He was a total "zero" by the natural yardstick. He began as an anti-Christian and then changed his mind, so he seemed to be politically wishy-washy. He fell out of public favor, and would have come out in the basement of any public-opinion polls if they'd had such polls then. He was the target of more than one assassination attempt. He had rotten luck with international transportation — he seemed to be jinxed, having been shipwrecked more than once. He was stoned by angry mobs and jailed by angry judges.

Paul had some problems in life!

As he sat in that damp, cold cell, chained to the wall, he must have thought back to his early days as a Pharisee, when he dedicated his workdays to murdering men and women of God.

He may even have felt that he was reaping what he had sown: persecution for persecution.

But Paul also realized God was using his problems for a purpose.

Even his prison terms were turned into times of magnificent inspiration.

Paul could have wallowed in self-pity as he paid his debts in that prison cell. But no. He insisted joyfully in one of his prison letters, "This one thing I do, forgetting those things which are behind, and reaching forth unto those things which are before, I press toward the mark for the prize of the high calling of God in Christ Jesus" (Philippians 3:13,14).

Paul's problems had a divine purpose. In his prison years, he wrote much of the New Testament under the direct guidance of God's Holy Spirit. Had he continued to preach and travel, he might never have had time to write so many of the books of the Bible which have blessed you and me.

Your problems also have a divine purpose. Even in the thick of your problems, your heavenly

Father wants to teach you to grow in His Word and His love.

In the following chapters of this book, I want to share with you a few ways you can begin to grow through your struggles in specific areas of your life.

Soon, with God's help, you will be well on your way to learning how to live life and love it.

4

THE KNOT AT THE END
OF THE ROPE

When God called me to leave my father and mother, my brother and sisters, and begin a new kind of ministry in Akron, Ohio, it was not an easy calling to accept.

I have often said that this was the most difficult decision I had to make in my life. I had known nothing but my family's ministry for over 30 years. I had managed my family's evangelistic outreach for over two decades. I had plunked my guitar and had sung along with my brother and sisters in almost every little town from one edge of the continent to the other. I had starved with them, wept with them, trusted God with them, overcome great struggles with them.

Even when I married Maude Aimee, we both went on with the Humbard Family Evangelistic Team, riding the old evangelistic circuit, preaching and praying for souls as best we knew how.

But now God had called me aside, away from the only life I'd ever known. He spoke to my heart as we came to our stop in Akron, Ohio, and directed me into a new ministry. It was a ministry so unusual that almost no one believed it was genuinely of the Lord. I was to stay in Akron, build a large church, and televise our services.

In 1952 this was unheard of. But there was more. The Lord also showed me, through the eye of faith, that I was to take our televised services into every state of the Union, and then into all the world. This was physically impossible, because even the great television networks of the United States had not yet been fully established. In fact, videotape, which the television industry uses almost exclusively today, had not been invented yet!

I spent weeks before the Lord desperately trying to make this once-in-a-lifetime decision. I had no money to start with. I had no church. I had no building. I had no congregation. How could this calling be right?

But the Holy Spirit kept confirming it in my heart. And eventually, along with Maude Aimee, my sister Leona, and her husband, Wayne Jones, I feebly launched our worldwide television ministry. I had only $65 in my pocket.

In the following days and weeks and months, and even years — as we built the Cathedral of Tomorrow, as we scratched for television equipment and struggled to get on the air — from that day on, there were thousands of opportunities to get depressed.

As I look over the history of our ministry, it is still just a string of impossible situations — one after another — and every obstacle was a good cause for depression.

Depression is one of the most universal problems facing people today.

More people write to me about this problem than any other problem of life: "I am depressed. I don't know why. Please help me."

You may have dozens of reasons to be depressed. You may be facing family problems, work problems, money problems; you may feel left out at your church or school or office or shop.

You may not even know what you're depressed about.

During some of my darkest days, as this ministry faced financial collapse, as we tried to build each new part of our worldwide outreach, I could have easily felt depressed. But there was something standing in the way which wouldn't allow me to slip into depression.

Something was standing in the gap, absorbing the tensions and disappointments like a dry sponge. That something was ... the seed of faith.

What is the seed of faith? It is the seed you have planted in God as you accept Him as your heavenly Father. Your seed of faith is planted in your own heart, as you invite Christ into your life. It is the basis, the foundation, the cornerstone, on which God builds your Christian life. As you plant that seed of faith, God nurtures and develops it into the fruit of the Spirit.

And that seed of faith stood in the way of any depression I might have felt. In spite of every setback I still had that little grain of faith, that tiny strand of hope that clings to God and says, "No matter what happens, I love you, and you are in charge of my life."

It was this seed of faith that Job displayed when he was down. "Though he slay me, yet will I trust in him" (Job 13:15) was how Job expressed his faith in God.

It is this seed of faith that trusts God to have a purpose in every problem.

It is this seed of faith that remembers, even in the bleakest hours, that God loves you and has promised that "I will never leave thee, nor forsake thee" (Hebrews 13:5).

It is this seed of faith that even in the most depressing moments would cause the apostle Paul to say that the "sufferings of this present time are not worthy to be compared with the glory which shall be revealed . . . " (Romans 8:18).

You might think of this seed of faith another way. Someone once said that when you are at the end of your rope, just tie a knot and hang on!

Faith is the knot at the end of the rope, that allows you to hang on even when you can't see the happy ending.

In fact, God tells us that faith is bound to be invisible. "Faith is . . . the evidence of things not seen" (Hebrews 11:1).

We trust in God through faith, even though we can't see how help can possibly be on the way.

The apostle Paul called it by another name. The "shield of faith" in Ephesians 6:16, is what he said we Christians should use to arm ourselves with, "above all." In other words, it is the most important thing a Christian has as he strives to live the Christ-life.

You may feel that your faith is weak, or that you have no faith at all.

But if you have accepted Jesus Christ as Saviour, you have already expressed your faith in Him, by believing in Him to cleanse you of your sins. The Bible says that God *gives* us — a measure of faith. It is given to all believers (Romans 12:3).

We don't have to beg God to give us faith — it's a gift that He freely gives us.

But we *can* pray for God to *strengthen* our faith. And He will honor our prayers.

It is God's responsibility to plant that "measure of faith" within us but it is our responsibility to grow a good crop of faith.

How can you grow a good crop of faith? That's the topic of the next chapter.

5

GROWING A GOOD CROP OF FAITH

Remember that everything in God's creation operates on the principle of seedtime and harvest. God told Noah after the flood, "While the earth remaineth, seedtime and harvest, and cold and heat, and summer and winter, and day and night shall not cease" (Genesis 8:22).

You reap what you sow. So you must plant the right seeds to grow a good crop of faith.

First, you can grow a good crop of faith by reading the Word of God. This is the most important part of growing a good crop of faith; faith in God grows as we learn to know God more intimately. Study your Bible. Seek God's wisdom as you read it. Pray that God will strengthen your faith and enlighten your understanding as you study the Scriptures. You will find your faith growing stronger every day (and depression will flee!).

It's a joy to know God's Word never changes. God's Word is settled and fixed (Psalm 119:89). You can stand on it, just as I have done all during the years I have faced great obstacles in our ministry. God's Word was settled and fixed in my heart, and never once did I think that our ministry would not succeed. God had spoken to me, He had strengthened my faith to believe in the vision He had given me. I trusted God to give the victory!

A short time ago one of the major religions of the world decided to rearrange their rules concerning the selection and qualifications of people to be leaders in their churches. Earlier, they had changed another rule, and before that they had changed yet another rule. Think how uncertain we would be if God's Word changed with each new age!

But God's Word never changes, because God's character never changes. He is "the same yesterday, and today, and for ever" (Hebrews 13:8).

So you can have faith that God will give you the victory!

Friend, I want to share with you this keynote passage of Scripture which will remind you every day of God's unchanging power.

"For though we walk in the flesh, we do not war after the flesh: (for

the weapons of our warfare are not carnal, but mighty through God to the pulling down of strongholds;) casting down imaginations, and every high thing that exalteth itself against the knowledge of God, and bringing into captivity every thought to the obedience of Christ" (II Corinthians 10:3-5).

Whenever you feel depression coming on, I want you to open your Bible and read those three verses. They are filled with the power of the almighty God. Mark them in your Bible so that they will always stand out for you. They are there to help you grow a good crop of faith.

Another way to grow a good crop of faith is to discover the power of prayer.

"The effectual fervent prayer of a righteous man availeth much," the Bible says (James 5:16).

Why should anybody pray? Because prayer is the greatest power in the universe. I've made our television ministry a prayer ministry since the very first day.

We've prayed for the salvation of lost souls and for the healing of the sick; we've prayed for God to bless our ministry and to work miracles when we've faced disaster.

A few years ago I went a step further. I formed the Prayer Key Family. First, I gathered my own family, and then I gathered our worldwide family of believers. Together each week, we all pray for the needs of those people who have written or called our ministry.

Our Prayer Key Family members do three things regularly: Pray for our ministry every day, fast for lost souls every week, give toward our television ministry each and every month. But the backbone of the Prayer Key Family is prayer.

How does prayer work?

Prayer puts God's power to work for you.

Near the end of the service one Sunday morning in the Cathedral of Tomorrow, I asked everyone with any kind of need to stand for prayer. Everyone in the church stood up! People were plugging into a power source greater than any government agency, greater than any amount of money, greater than any power source in this world. They were putting God's power to work for them.

Then I asked everyone to remain standing who was unsure of his soul's salvation, or had not yet made a public profession of his faith in Christ Jesus. I was amazed at the number of people who remained standing for this prayer. I was glad they did, because they were also *securing* their connection to the power source.

44

They were making sure they were connected to God's divine power in their lives.

After the service a couple from Quebec came up to me in the church lobby. They were glowing with joy, like thousand-watt light bulbs.

"This is the greatest day of our lives!" the man told me excitedly. "We have watched your services on television, and we have attended a church in our community. We've prayed with you for forgiveness of our sins during your television program, and we've dedicated our lives to the Lord.

"But before today," the man went on, "we had never made a public profession of our faith in Jesus Christ. We will never be the same!"

That man declared that he and his wife would never be the same.

But exactly *how* were they *different?* They had plugged into God's power source in faith, and they had secured that connection by publicly professing their faith, which had in turn strengthened their faith.

Now the next time that couple runs into a battle, the next time something happens in their lives that threatens to depress them — when those thousand-watt light bulbs grow dim — they're going to be able to hold onto that seed of faith. And the next time they feel God doesn't love them, they're going to be strong enough in their faith to know that "His grace is sufficient" (II Corinthians 12:9).

45

Because they are growing a good crop of faith, they're going to be able to tie a knot in the end of the rope and hang on.

God's Word tells us, "Cast thy burden upon the Lord, and He shall sustain thee" (Psalm 55:22).

What will He sustain you for? Do you need to be sustained through the sunshine? Do you need to be strengthened during the "glory-hallelujah" times? Or do you need to be protected and fortified during the storms of life, when you feel as if you are under attack?

Plug into God as your power source, and secure your connection to that source of power. It will strengthen your faith, and help you to live life — and love it!

6

PRAYING NONSTOP

Your prayertimes are also a key to that good crop of faith.

What exactly is prayer?

Prayer is not just something you do.

If it were simply an activity, it would be impossible to obey the commandment to "Pray without ceasing" (I Thessalonians 5:17).

Instead, prayer is an attitude. Prayer is a lifestyle. The Bible doesn't say prayer is just an activity with any certain rules to follow; it does say prayer is the sincere desire of the heart making its requests known unto God (Philippians 4:6-8).

So, when I get up every day and prepare myself for

the task God has given me to do through our television ministry, *that's my prayer*. When I went to that Cleveland, Ohio, television station 13 times to get our programs on the air decades ago, *that was my prayer*. When I wept before a television audience because our ministry faced financial struggles when we were building the Cathedral of Tomorrow and our television ministry, *that was my prayer*.

Everything you do that reflects the "sincere desire of the heart" is a prayer to God.

This is how you can accomplish the apostle Paul's instruction to "pray without ceasing" (I Thessalonians 5:17).

I knew a pastor in Detroit who spent six hours studying the Word and six hours praying every day. This was a beautiful expression of his dedication to God, but his church was not growing.

If I'd been that pastor I think I might have spent my time a little differently. It might have been better to study three hours, pray three hours, and then spend six hours visiting the sick, counseling people with problems, and putting all that devotion into action.

That pastor may have been praying all six of those hours every day for his church to grow. But those prayers were not being answered. Why not?

Because prayer is not just something you say or something you think.

Prayer is action.

Prayer is putting shoe leather on your sermons —

getting out and loving people. Your personal calendar is a prayer, because the way you use your time is a prayer.

When you sing the praises of God, *that's your prayer*. When you fellowship over a meal, *that's a prayer*.

A preacher was once asked to speak at a convention on the subject of praying without ceasing. He was nervous about it.

"How am I going to speak on that verse?" he asked his wife as he sat in his study at the church. "Nobody really prays without ceasing!"

A little elderly lady overhead them and interrupted with a big smile.

"Oh, yes, pastor, I do," she said. "I have for years. When I wake up in the morning I say, 'Lord, thank you for this day you've given me. Let the light of God shine through me.' Then as I wash my face I say, 'Lord, cleanse me with your heavenly soap and water.' Then as I get dressed I say, 'Lord, clothe me with robes of righteousness.' Then as I build the fire in the fireplace I say, 'Lord, kindle the fire of your Holy Spirit in me.' Then — "

"That's enough," the pastor said. "I think I can preach that sermon now!"

You also pray a prayer on paper every week — in your checkbook.

Your checkbook is a prayer because it reflects your desires, your priorities, your attitudes.

Remember, prayer is the "sincere desire" of the

heart. If your checkbook reveals faithfulness to God's work, *that's your prayer.* If it reveals selfishness, then that's what you're seeking, and *that's your prayer.*

Are your desires right? Your checkbook is a prayer on paper that gives you the answer to that question.

Your desires infiltrate everything you do, everything you think, everything you feel. Before you can discover the power of prayer, you must examine your motives and desires. Are they pure? Do they represent the prayer you want to make known to God?

And there is one more key ingredient to growing a good crop of faith . . .

7

THE WASTE OF WORRY

Commitment to God's will is another key ingredient to growing a good crop of faith.

Committing your life to God's will is not just a vague theory that you can shrug and agree with; but it is a thing you must do deliberately as an act of your will every time you face a battle. If you can learn the secret of commitment to God's will, you will have taken a giant step toward learning to live life and love it.

When my dad died at the age of 69, I wondered why it had happened. I needed him around. I missed him. Things were happening in this ministry and around the Cathedral. This church had only been open a year and we were just beginning to reach across the North American continent with the television programs. I wished my dad could see all the exciting things that were happening and share in the joy of them. He had talked about someday visiting Jerusalem, but he never got to go. There was so much that dad missed because God took him home.

But God was through with my dad on this earth. His ministry here was over. The heavenly Father only had my dad on a 52-year preaching schedule, and then he was done. It was over.

I had a natural urge to question God's judgment. It didn't seem fair. It didn't seem right. I didn't understand the reason for dad's death.

But every problem has a purpose, even if we don't understand that purpose.

We may never understand God's purpose until we get to heaven. But we can be sure God has a purpose, because we are *committed to His will*. That's the secret of commitment to God's will: turning the problem over to Him when we cannot understand *why*.

I've seen people question God's sovereign wisdom when they don't understand why something is happening.

But when you question God, you are saying, "Maybe I know more than God does about this situation."

This is impossible, for God knows all things! Remember, God loves you and won't let any problem overtake you. But you must commit yourself to God's will.

I met some ladies in a restaurant not long ago — one who was soon to have her first baby, and the other who was going to be the baby's grandma. The expectant mother was 33 years old, and the women were worried about complications in the pregnancy.

I prayed with them right there in the restaurant. When I finished, they were crying. "Do you have a good doctor?" I asked the mother-to-be.

She said yes.

"Well, if I had a broken arm," I told her, "I'd go to a good doctor that I had confidence in, and I'd have him set that bone in place. Then I'd leave it in God's hands to heal that break, because I would have done all I could.

"Now that's what you should do, too," I told the ladies. "You've done all you can; now commit yourself to God. He's your partner. You don't need to leave this restaurant crying — go out smiling!"

And they did. They decided to follow a formula for living life and loving it.

When you face a problem, first pray, and then commit it to God.

Can you do any more than this? No, even when you've done all you can in your own strength, God is still in control.

And then worrying becomes a waste!

When you worry, you are saying, "God, I'm afraid you can't do it. I'm afraid you're not going to give your very best for me. Heavenly Father, I don't trust you."

Is that the prayer you want to pray? Of course not. But that is the prayer that worry prays. When you worry, you are putting the burden back on your own shoulders, instead of "casting all your cares on Him" (I Peter 5:7). When you worry, you assume responsibility for something that is supposed to be God's responsibility.

When you commit a problem to God, you are asking Him to take care of it. But worry brings that problem back to your own doorstep.

Imagine what would happen if I asked my brother-in-law, Wayne Jones, to go to Africa for me, to make all the preparations for a rally we were going to hold there — and then I sat at home in Akron all the time he was gone and worried whether Wayne was doing everything right.

In the first place, it would be silly to worry about Wayne. He's been doing this sort of thing for me — and more — for over a quarter-century.

And, by the same token, it's silly to worry about God caring for you. He's been in this business since time began!

But I also don't want to worry about Wayne taking care of the rally planning because that wastes my time in Akron. The reason I send Wayne ahead is so I can *keep on ministering* while the problems are being worked out. If I spend all my time worrying about Wayne, I might as well go to Africa myself and make rally plans. Worry wastes the time I can spend ministering.

And when *you* worry, friend, you're wasting the time God gave you that you could be spending in ministry to others, in ministry to the Lord, in your own personal ministry. When you commit a problem to the Lord, it frees you to go on living a Christian life, effectively, in His kingdom. You can live a life that will be a blessing to others, a life that will be worry-free and full of personal ministry.

That's why commitment to God's will is so important.

God will take care of your problems according to His own perfect will, if you will only commit them to Him. That means: "let your problems go."

"I will never leave thee, nor forsake thee" (Hebrews 13:5) Jesus says. Believe that He means what He says.

Trust in God's will. Trust in His character. Trust Him to love you enough to solve your problems. "Thou wilt keep him in perfect peace," the Bible says, "whose mind is stayed on thee: because he trusteth in thee" (Isaiah 26:3).

8

"How do you spell relief?"

GUILTY AS CHARGED

When I was in junior high school in Hot Springs, Arkansas, we had a place called the Manual Training Room. It was the same thing as a shop class in today's junior high schools. It is a place where youngsters can learn to use their hands to make things out of metal and wood.

There are always dozens of favorite things to work with in such a shop, and I had my favorite in that Manual Training Room.

It was a set of metal stamps, one for every letter of the alphabet. They were the kind you'd tap on one end to engrave the letter into the surface you were working on.

One day those metal stamps got the better of me and I took three very special ones out of the box — the three that spelled REX. Other boys in the Manual Training Room had taken other letters, so the set was already incomplete. Who would miss three more? I didn't expect Mr. Stephens, the shop teacher, to come after me.

And he didn't.

I got away with my little crime.

I felt a little guilty, but pretty soon I forgot about it.

But it so happened that within a few weeks I accepted Jesus Christ as my personal Saviour. I was sitting in my father's church, listening to one of his straight-talk sermons, when the convicting power of the Holy Spirit fell upon me — speaking to my heart about my need for salvation and the forgiveness that only Christ can give. I went to my dad's altar and fell on my knees and asked Jesus to come into my heart.

And it wasn't long before I remembered those metal stamps I had taken. It almost seemed like those three letters were calling out my name — "REX . . . REX . . . "

What I was feeling was *guilt*. It wasn't too good a feeling, and I wanted to get rid of it.

I scooped those three metal stamps into my pocket and headed straight for the Manual Training Room.

Now I could have sneaked those three stamps back into the box. Mr. Stephens would never have known I did anything wrong.

But I went straight to him. I was a baby Christian, and I didn't know a lot of deep theological principles, but even at the age of 13 I could tell there was a value in *restitution*.

So I said, "Mr. Stephens, I took these three metal stamps. I didn't ask your permission, and I didn't tell you I took them.

"But the other night," I told him, "I accepted Jesus

Christ as my personal Saviour, and I asked Him to forgive me of my sins. Now I'm here to return these stamps and make it up to you and take whatever punishment you want to give me."

What good does it do to make restitution? What good does it do to pay back your debts?

Mr. Stephens was surprised that I had come to him. He didn't punish me.

"You've already punished yourself, Rex," he said to me. He could tell I was feeling guilty.

But that *restitution* — that *paying back* — made an impact on Mr. B. G. Stephens. I visited Hot Springs 25 years later and saw Mr. Stephens again for the first time in all those years. And he still remembered that simple little act of restitution.

"From that day till this," Mr. Stephens said, "I knew Rex was conscientious. I've watched Rex on TV all these years. I've always had faith in that boy since then."

That simple act of restitution was the strongest sermon I ever preached to B. G. Stephens.

Restitution is a witness of Christ. It tells the world that Christ lives within you, that Christ is guiding your thoughts and your attitudes. That simple witness may make the difference in leading someone to Christ!

But what made me return those stamps at all? What

feeling was I responding to?

It was guilt.

Every person alive has felt guilty at least once. The Bible says, "For all have sinned, and come short of the glory of God" (Romans 3:23). And that feeling of guilt always follows sin.

Why? What is guilt? When it comes from God it is the signal God has planted inside of you to tell you that you have sinned or done wrong.

Guilty feelings are really a good thing when you think of them as a reminder from the Holy Spirit.

If you cut your bare foot on a piece of glass, but you don't feel any pain, you might bleed to death before you find out there is any problem! Pain serves a good purpose!

So do guilty feelings. They are a different kind of pain — the kind that says you are bleeding spiritually. When you feel guilty you are feeling the convicting power of the Holy Spirit working in your heart. It's a healthy urge to make the wrong *right*.

But the feeling of guilt, just like pain, is an uncomfortable thing. God has designed you *not* to enjoy it and not to tolerate it. Something inside you makes you want to be free of guilt. It tells you to cleanse yourself somehow.

That's the key question:

How do I get rid of this feeling of guilt?

Ultimately, the only way to get rid of *guilty feelings* is to get rid of the *guilt* itself. They are two different things.

Guilt is a fact. It is your sin. Because we all have sinned, we all share in the guilt for our sins. You have guilt; you are guilty. And guilt can only be redeemed by the saving power of Jesus Christ.

That's why we must ask forgiveness. That's how God cleanses us of our guilt. It's just as if the judge in the courtroom has dismissed the charges.

So, the first step toward getting rid of your guilty feelings is to ask God to forgive you.

Every sin breaks the relationship between you and your heavenly Father. First, you must restore that relationship. You may not have accepted Jesus Christ as your own personal Saviour. If that is the case, your guilt will keep on nagging at you until you make a decision either to accept or reject Christ. My prayer for you is that you will say yes to Jesus.

Then, if you have sinned against someone and they are hurting because of it, you have also broken your relationship with that person, and you must go to him and ask his forgiveness. This lets a double healing take place: it heals the hurt in that person, and it heals your feelings of guilt at the same time. And the relationship between the two of you is restored. This fulfills God's commandment to "Love thy neighbor as

61

thyself" (Romans 13:9), and you will be blessed for your obedience to God's Word.

And finally, make restitution if you can. When Jesus entered Zacchaeus' life, that dishonest little tax collector went back to all the people he had cheated and repaid them all four times what he had taken from them. Then Zacchaeus went a step further: he gave half of all his worldly goods to the poor people of the city.

Restitution helps the wounds of a broken relationship or a ruined testimony heal faster.

Sometimes, though, restitution is impossible. You can't give back lost years. In 1946, when I was only 27, a lady came up to me after one of my dad's hell-or-holiness sermons on a Sunday morning.

"My daughter and I have been on the outs for a long, long time," she told me with tears in her eyes. "I don't like her husband, and I didn't want her to marry him in the first place. So my daughter and I haven't spoken a word to each other in years.

"But I know I've been wrong," the lady went on. "I love my daughter, and this afternoon I'm asking my husband to drive me the 150 miles to her house to ask her forgiveness. Will you pray for me?"

I prayed that the daughter and her husband would have open hearts when the mother arrived.

Later that afternoon, the mother knocked on her daughter's door. Inside, she spilled out her hurts and asked her daughter and son-in-law to forgive her. Together the three of them cried and prayed and laughed through the afternoon, as the walls between them came tumbling down.

Before long the mother's husband had accepted Christ as his personal Saviour. He had seen the woman's bitterness all through the years, and even though she went to church faithfully, he did not see Christ in her because of that barrier. Now that this barrier was broken, the man could see the love of Jesus Christ, and he wanted the same thing in his own heart.

That woman had stood in the way of her husband's salvation all those years!

I learned a few things from that episode, and I've jotted them down in the next chapter . . .

9

GOD'S WILL, UNLIMITED

The healing of that bitter woman and her family taught me some lessons. First, I learned that I can follow the letter of the law and still neglect the spirit of the law. And I can go to heaven that way, but I will never have any power or influence as a Christian witness here on earth.

I also learned that I need to practice everyday Christianity. I learned that church-going is not enough. If I'm going to be a witness of Christ's love in the world I will have to practice Christian principles in every part of my life all through the week and in all my dealings with my family and friends and co-workers on the job. Otherwise, no one will have confidence in my testimony.

And I learned that restitution is as important as repentance. I can be sorry for my sin and God will forgive me. But until I *act* and make restitution to the person I've hurt, I'm never going to be completely healed of the guilty feelings inside.

I used to think it takes a great person to ask forgiveness and make restitution. But I've seen that God doesn't expect us to be any more than humans.

If you rely on Him to give you strength He will help you obey His own principles!

That's what that mother did when she came to me for prayer. She felt guilty. She knew she had to obey the Spirit within her and make things right with her daughter. But she didn't have the strength to do it herself. So she sought help.

When she united with another believer in prayer, this strengthened her faith. She had discovered the power of prayer.

She was putting God's power to work for her.

And when she plugged into that power source, she found she could do what she was supposed to do. She was not trying to operate under her own power; she was operating under God's power.

And you can, too.

That's why I encourage people to join with me and my family in the Prayer Key Family.

In this body of believers all around the world, we fortify each other's faith through the constant uplifting of each other's needs in prayer.

Every day the Prayer Key Family members pray for souls around the world.

Every week each member may fast a meal and spend that mealtime in prayer for the worldwide television ministry and for lost souls.

And each week at prayertime, during our television program, all the Prayer Key Family members in the world gather by way of television to pray specifically that God will answer the prayers and meet the needs of *every person who has written or called our ministry with a prayer request* during that week.

Even the simple act of writing that letter is an act of faith, because it says that you believe God can help you.

As we unite in this body of believers, we strengthen our faith and fortify our prayers, and we see God answering prayer every single week!

But our Prayer Key Family can't pray for your needs unless you send them to me.

When your letter arrives, I make sure that it is represented on our Prayer Table the very next time we gather for prayer. God tells us in His Word that "Where two or three are gathered together in my name, there am I in the midst of them" (Matthew 18:20). So we know God is listening when we join together in prayer each week!

That's why I want you to write me and send me your

prayer needs. Because God has promised to be there and meet our needs when we pray together.

If you don't act in faith and share your needs, you tie God's hands.

The Bible says that it is *not* God's will that any should perish (II Peter 3:9).

But there is often a failure on man's part to act in faith. It *is* God's will that every soul be saved, "that thou mayest prosper and be in health" (III John:2).

But God limits himself to the faith of His people. When you fail to act on faith, God does not act.

God's work in your life is limited by your faith.

Why do you have to *act* in faith? Because as the Scripture says, "For as the body without the spirit is dead, so faith without works is dead also" (James 2:26).

Write out your needs. Be specific and share them with others.

"Ye have not, because ye ask not" (James 4:2).

But when we ask, God has promised to answer. "Pray one for another, that ye may be healed" (James 5:16).

I see a world full of Christian weaklings today.

A Christian weakling is what I call a person who has accepted Christ as Saviour but has never learned the secret of growing in God. He may be well on his way to heaven, but he has failed to live a powerful, effective Christian life. He has never discovered the power of prayer. He has never worked to build up his faith. He is still a baby Christian, still bound up by guilty feelings, still wasting his life in worry.

Perhaps your guilty feelings may follow you even after you are no longer guilty!

You may sense a nagging uneasiness. Why?

Maybe you have not accepted God's forgiveness in faith. The apostle Paul reminds us, however, that "There is therefore now no condemnation to them which are in Christ Jesus" (Romans 8:1). Accept God's forgiveness and "put on the new man" (Ephesians 4:24). If you don't accept His forgiveness in faith you are saying, "Lord, I don't believe you have really done what you promised."

It's tragic that some Christians are still weaklings even many years after they accept Christ. But there is always hope.

It's never too late to begin growing in the Lord.

And that's what I'm praying for you — that you will open your heart to the leading of the Holy Spirit and grow in God's power. Put your sins and your guilt behind you by asking forgiveness and making restitution. Grow a good, healthy crop of faith by digging into God's Word and discovering the power of prayer.

"But without faith it is impossible to please him: for he that cometh to God must believe," the Bible says, " . . . that he is a rewarder of them that diligently seek him" (Hebrews 11:6).

Grow a good crop of faith. It is one giant step toward living life and loving it.

10

FEAST IN THE VALLEY

Why is it so important to grow a good crop of faith? Because Satan wants to slip in and plant weeds at every opportunity. He wants to choke out the good in you and introduce the bad.

But a healthy crop of faith will withstand any attack of Satan.

A good crop of faith will give you confidence as a Christian. It will not let you be shaken when you are tempted, and it will not let you doubt your salvation when you give in to temptation. I've known people to go nearly crazy with fear over their soul's state just because they spoke an unkind word to someone or slipped into some sin of that sort.

But there are two kinds of sin, and a Christian growing a good crop of faith can recognize the difference.

One kind of sin is the damning kind.

This is the sin that can keep you out of heaven. If you refuse to accept Christ as your personal Saviour and die, you will be cast into eternal darkness because of that damning sin in your life.

But there are other sins that even Christians commit every day.

You may fail to pray faithfully. You may speak unkindly to your neighbor. You may cut a corner on your tax records or keep a cashier's overpayment to yourself. These are indeed sins, but you are not doomed to hell because of them. God's love "covers a multitude of sins" (I Peter 4:8). And the words of Romans 8:1 assure you that as long as you love Jesus — as long as you are "in Christ Jesus" — there is "no condemnation in you."

God still loves you.

Only if you reject His son will He keep you out of heaven.

Of course, you will still feel guilty because your sins, no matter how small, still make you guilty. And every debt must be paid. You may still suffer because of your sins.

One of the most dangerous things about giving in to gossip or anger or one of these sins is:

**It opens the door for the enemy
of your soul to attack you in your
weakened condition.**

The more like Jesus you can be in every detail of
your life, the less likely you will be to eventually fall
away and backslide, rejecting Jesus altogether.

While I was growing up, many religious groups
were trying to promote an extremist doctrine that
made people believe every time they did something
sinful they had lost their salvation. They were asking
Jesus back into their hearts every time they said something unkind.

But what this doctrine really says is, "If I'm good
enough, I'll go to heaven." And that idea is false
because no person is good enough to reach heaven.

**We don't reach heaven by way of
our goodness. We reach heaven
by way of our faith.**

Only a right relationship with Jesus Christ will get
you into heaven.

Your strong faith does, however, help you do what
you can to live a Christian life. God has given you the
will to do right or wrong, and it's up to you to make
those decisions.

**A good crop of faith helps you
make the best decisions in every
area of your life.**

Faith helps you go the extra mile as a witness for
Jesus Christ.

Faith is what helps you resist the temptation to cheat on your income taxes.

Faith is what reminds you in an angry moment that backbiting is sinful, not just ugly.

Faith is what gives you the power to say, "I'm sorry,"

Faith is what gives you what you need to "cleanse yourself from all filthiness of the flesh and spirit" (II Corinthians 7:1).

Many people have asked me to pray about their habits: alcohol, tobacco, and so forth. And I do pray for them. But actually, God gives *you* the power to cut your bad habits short. God will help you, as you center your thoughts on Jesus Christ. But you have developed your habits as an act of your free will, and God will not impose upon that will — because your will is something He gave you, to use however you wish.

That's why you must decide how your life will be lived. If you decide to make Christ the focus of your thoughts and actions, God will strengthen your faith and help you in times of trouble. If you decide against Christ, you are on your own.

Of course, there are bound to be times in even the Christian's life when sin slips in.

There are bound to be troubled times, doubting times — but those are the times that God uses to make our lives rich.

Not long ago my daughter Elizabeth told our television audience about her own mountaintop experiences. She had been on real mountaintops in Europe before. She found even though they were beautiful from a distance, they were usually barren or snow-covered by the time she got up to them.

The valleys are where the fruits and vegetables grow.

"That's where the real feeding takes place," she pointed out. "And that is where the real growth takes place."

To grow, we must go through the valleys. The mountaintops alone are not enough.

11

REFORM SCHOOL

A man came to the Cathedral one day to talk over his problems with me. He had been a member of a church in another city, but the people had taken his name off the membership rolls and expelled him from their worship.

"Why?" I asked him as he sat unhappily in my office.

Then the man told me a fascinating story.

He was praying one day alone in his home, when suddenly he heard thunder. In the middle of flashes of lightning, he saw Jesus in a vision before his eyes. He fell on the floor before the Lord, worshipping.

The next Sunday morning he asked his pastor if he could have the pulpit for a few moments to share something of a very important nature with the congregation. The pastor consented, and the man proceeded to tell the church about his incredible vision, urging them to seek the same experience.

Now he sat sadly in my office, banished like an ugly dog with fleas.

"Do you believe my vision was real?" he asked forlornly.

"Well, maybe it was, maybe it wasn't," I responded. "If it was, then I praise the Lord for your experience. But it's *yours.*"

The man looked at me with a quizzical expression. "What do you mean?"

"That experience was something given to *you*," I replied. "It wasn't given to me. It wasn't given to your pastor or anyone else in your church. If that experience edified you or strengthened your faith, fine. But it was given to you alone. And some things are better kept to yourself."

The man paused a moment.

"I never thought about it like that before," he said quietly. "I expected you to throw me out, just like my own pastor did."

"Maybe I would have," I told him, "if I hadn't been around so long. But I've seen hundreds of people come and go with unusual experiences. And I just tell every one of them,

'Praise the Lord for your experience, but don't ask *me* to have *your* experience.' "

Then I asked the man, "If someone had told you a year ago you were going to have this vision, you would have thought they were crazy, wouldn't you?"

He nodded, grinning.

"Now there are diversities of gifts, but the same

Spirit . . . but all these worketh that one and the selfsame Spirit, dividing to every man severally as he will" (I Corinthians 12:4,11).

That man was, for the first time, learning that life is not a reform school.

The man was insisting on molding others into his own shape exactly — something that God does not even do Himself!

You may feel pressured by other people, perhaps your own relatives, who do not match the pattern you have established for your life. You may feel the urge to force them into your mold. But God has a different plan.

I once knew of a church where the men of the church began setting aside Saturday evenings for prayer in the church basement, followed by personal visitation and witnessing. The Lord began to bless them beautifully. The fruits of their labors increased. Some of the people in the church said the deacons were getting a little "spiritual."

Finally it was reported that some of the deacons were praying in tongues in the Saturday night prayer meetings.

This was just too much for one gentleman in the church. He stormed into the pastor's study, demanding to know what the pastor was going to do about it.

The pastor responded calmly,

"Well, I reckon since I had nothing to do *with* it, I'll have

nothing to do *about* it."

That pastor was following a principle of leadership which is also a principle of life. And it applies to you and me every day of our lives. That principle, if every Christian were to follow it, would unite the denominations of the world into a single vibrant body of believers, all worshipping and working for the kingdom of Jesus Christ without competing over the fine points of doctrine.

This is the principle of affirmation, which is just a big word that means acting positively instead of negatively.

It means leaving room for the other guy. It means letting God do the work. That man with a vision had approached his church wanting to *reform* them, or change them. But God has a Holy Spirit that is marvelously equipped to do that kind of work. And the Holy Spirit never reforms the person. He *influences* the heart.

The gentleman who was unhappy with the charismatic men's meeting wanted to reform them, to make the men over in his own image. But God didn't design people to accept reform. He gave us a will which makes up its own mind. God puts you in charge of yourself, by giving you a will and setting it free. You have a free will.

But He also gave you a heart. Your heart is capable of being moved, capable of loving, of being loved, of hurting.

And the Holy Spirit pursues your heart.

The Holy Spirit moves gently in your heart, speaking words of love and tenderly persuading you.

That's the only way a human being full of sin and anger and problems can open himself to the love of God.

So how can you change someone's mind? You can't.

You can't impose your will on anybody. Their will is their own, just as your will is your own. You can't make anyone experience your vision. You can't make anyone speak in tongues or quit speaking in tongues.

I never saved a soul in my life. I never healed a body or mended a marriage. I couldn't if I wanted to. It's not my business. It's God's.

My only business is telling people about Jesus Christ.

I'm in sales, not management.

Once I fulfill my responsibility to share the good news, my audience is in God's hands. I can't impose my will on anyone.

And neither will God. God doesn't impose His will on anyone. He leaves your will alone. He limits Himself to your heart. He will love you and speak to you, but He will never force you.

To form a happy relationship with anyone else — from your mother-in-law to your boss to your butcher

81

— follow the principle of affirmation.

Act positively, not negatively.

Leave room for that person to do as *he* chooses. You don't have to do as he does; but let the Holy Spirit do any work that needs to be done in him.

But the secret ingredient of this principle is not found in watching the person who bothers you. Instead, the key is in watching *yourself!* It seems backwards, but this is how Christ always taught the people while He was ministering here on earth.

When the woman caught in adultery was brought to Him, that sin must have bothered Jesus, for His Spirit was troubled by any sinfulness.

But Jesus taught affirmation, not reformation. He turned to the people who were feeling bothered, not to the person who was bothering them! He looked at the angry crowd and said, "He that is without sin among you, let him first cast a stone at her" (John 8:7).

By the same token, when someone is bothering you — when you are angry or indignant or hurt or disgusted — look at yourself, instead of at the other person.

Then ask yourself these questions.

1. **Am I without sin in my own life?**
2. **Am I guilty of doing the same kind of thing that I see the**

other person doing?

3. Is there anything in my life that I can change to make the situation more comfortable?
4. How can I *minister* to that person? Am I obeying God's law of giving and receiving? Am I giving in order to receive?

The final question is the key one.

Jesus never seemed to focus on a person's crimes. He knew every person's sins, but He always looked at how a person was hurting *because* of the sins.

That's why Jesus always forgave a person's sins when they came to Him with a problem. Because He knew that sin hurts.

Jesus saw people as bundles of needs, not bundles of sins.

And that's our example. When your mother-in-law irritates you by suggesting a different tablecloth for the dining room, ask yourself, "How can I meet her needs?" In that perspective you may soon see how insignificant your own anger really is.

God's way is selfless. You soon forget about grasping at your own happiness and comfort, and you start concentrating on giving of yourself to others as Jesus did

This is perhaps one of the strangest keys to living life and loving it . . . the great paradox of giving in order to receive.

12

THE GREAT PARADOX

Friend, I want the coming days of your life to be the greatest you've ever lived. I want you to be happy and fulfilled and feeling rich. I want you to live life and love it.

But Christianity is a great paradox. Jesus said you only find life if you lose your life (Matthew 10:39). You only find happiness if you forget about your own happiness. You get by giving, not by getting.

It doesn't make sense to the rational mind. We've distorted God's law of giving and receiving. We pursue happiness and wonder why we feel unhappy. The suicide rate goes up and up. The divorce rate does likewise. Child abuse has become an epidemic.

Why? Because we try to *get* happiness. We want to be given to. And all the while, Jesus is saying, "You've got it backwards! If you give of yourself, then you will receive richly!"

Selflessness is the heart of your Christianity.

That's the foundation of our Prayer Key Family. When I first gathered our worldwide Prayer Key Family together through television, I stressed the idea of selflessness — God's law of giving and receiving. When you pray for our ministry every day as a member of the Prayer Key Family, you are giving of yourself to God — giving of your time and energy and prayers. But God doesn't let you give for nothing. He is a debtor to no man. He blesses you for your giving.

When you fast one meal a week for lost souls as a member of the Prayer Key Family, you are giving of yourself to God — and God will bless you for your giving.

When you give faithfully each month to support our television ministry to the lost of the world, you are giving of yourself to God — and God will bless you for your giving.

Pastor Cho Yonggi of the world's largest church in Seoul, South Korea, says, "The hardest thing for me to do is to be poor. I give away my money to the Lord's work more and more so that I ought to be poor. But God keeps giving me back more than I give to Him and I just keep getting richer and richer!"

This is God's law of giving and receiving in action.

It doesn't apply just to money. It applies to anything you give to God — your time, your energy, your attention, your material possessions, your special talents and abilities. I encourage people to give away what they have, because I know God will honor the principle of seedtime and harvest, His law of giving and receiving, and bless them more abundantly for their giving!

People sometimes wonder why I don't apologize for asking our television viewers to give financial support to our worldwide ministry. But it would be wrong of me *not* to ask you to give. God only blesses what He possesses.

So you can only be blessed to the extent that you give to God.

If I didn't give you an opportunity to give, I would be failing to give you an opportunity to be blessed!

Jesus met a rich young man one day who was looking for happiness. He had kept all of the Ten Commandments, but he had not yet discovered how to live life and love it. He was worried about dying. He was searching for the key to eternal life in order to find some peace here on earth.

Jesus gave him strange instructions. "Sell all that thou hast," He said, "and distribute unto the poor, and thou shalt have treasure in heaven" (Luke 18:22).

This was God's law of giving and receiving in action. Jesus was simply telling the rich young man that he would have to give in order to receive.

The followers of Jesus had already seen this principle at work many times. The one leper who paused to give thanks was made whole (Luke 17:19).

The father who went the extra mile, even in the face of failure, saw a son delivered from demon possession (Luke 9:42).

The miracle of the loaves and fishes demonstrated the principle of giving and receiving (Luke 9:17).

The sick little woman, who had spent her life's savings on doctors, pushed through the rowdy crowd to receive her healing (Luke 8:47).

Even a woman full of sin, who gave of herself to the worship of Jesus, was completely forgiven (Luke 7:48).

But this rich young man didn't trust the law of giving and receiving.

He couldn't stand to risk his material possessions. He didn't trust God to give him back more than he gave to God. He didn't believe in the principle of seedtime and harvest.

And so, instead of learning how to live life and love it, the young man, as rich as he was, went away "very sorrowful" (Luke 18:23).

I never ask for something our ministry doesn't need. But I never fail to ask, for I would fail in my responsibility as a minister if I did.

Giving is a key to receiving.

"For whatsoever a man soweth," the Bible says, "that shall he also reap" (Galatians 6:7).

Learn to give. If you aren't tithing, start now. This is a scriptural principle that sets aside ten percent of your income for God's work.

If you are tithing, learn to step up in your giving. Learn to test God's promise of blessing by increasing your giving.

This is the only promise of God's Word that challenges you to test it:

"Prove me now herewith, saith the Lord of hosts, if I will not open you the windows of heaven, and pour you out a blessing, that there shall not be room enough to receive it" (Malachi 3:10).

But God's law of giving and receiving works in every situation. As you face any problem in your life, ask yourself,

"Am I giving of myself to receive a blessing in the face of this problem?"

If you focus on how to *give* rather than how to *get* happiness, you'll be well on your way to living life and loving it.

13

"I do."

LIFE IN THE
PRESSURE COOKER

The family setting is probably the one place where God's law of giving and receiving needs to be most faithfully employed.

The home is a pressure cooker in many ways, where people spend so much time together that their inhibitions drop, tempers often flare, disagreements fan into fights, resentments build up silently over the weeks.

Still, this is only mankind's version of the home.

The home is God's greatest institution on earth.

He created it as a model of happiness and fulfillment. It is a miniature version of the body of Christ, where one member relies on the other and vice versa, where each gives to the next, and by that process everybody's needs are supplied.

Our human nature, however, doesn't normally like that arrangement. In our natural selfishness, we don't like to be relied on to supply the needs of other body members or family members.

We don't naturally like depending on someone else, either. We would rather be our own bosses, controlling our own destinies ("Mother! I'd rather do it myself!").

That's why understanding and practicing the principle of seedtime and harvest — God's law of giving and receiving — in the home is so important. In fact, it's second in importance only to salvation itself.

A man's first duty is to love God. His second duty is to establish a God-loving home.

With those two duties accomplished, every other element of life falls more neatly into place.

When a person comes to me with a problem, the first question I ask him is, "What is standing between you and God?"

If there's nothing blocking the relationship with your heavenly Father then the next question is, "What is standing between you and your family?"

The solution to almost every problem lies in the answer to one of those two simple questions.

Very recently a businessman flew into Akron from New York to meet with me on a Saturday. It was an important meeting, and Saturday was the only day I had free.

"This is rare for me," he said that day. "I almost

never conduct business on weekends. My job keeps me traveling a lot, and I'm hardly ever home during the week; so my Sundays are devoted to the Lord, and my Saturdays are devoted to my family."

The man has two Sabbaths — the Lord's Day on Sunday and the Family's Day on Saturday.

I admire that kind of dedication. That businessman is obeying the principle of seedtime and harvest with his family — sowing seeds faithfully every weekend to reap a harvest of happiness in his home.

He is busy enough that he could easily say, "I don't have time for my wife and my children." But he makes time. He gives to his family. Every Saturday is seedtime, and harvestime will go on continually because of it.

What are your priorities in life?

Is your first priority making money? Are you primarily interested in your new car? Does your job occupy your mind every minute of every day?

Examine your priorities right now. Your first priority must be your relationship with God, and your second priority must be your relationship with your family. Everything else can take its place below them on the list.

Why is the home so important to a happy life?

Because God designed the home as the cornerstone of life on earth. If the home fails, the community fails. If the community fails, the state fails. And the entire world follows suit. It is Satan's grandest and ugliest scheme.

We have already seen it beginning to happen. The divorce rate is climbing. Child abuse and wife-beating incidences are skyrocketing in frequency.

And now cities are struggling to survive. With the rising crime rates and sagging morale, city dwellers are fleeing in huge numbers — which shrinks the tax base, lowers school enrollments, decreases the community's need for businesses and services, throws out hundreds of jobs, and pushes the city to the brink of bankruptcy.

The state struggles to keep people in its cities above water, and nation after nation staggers under the burden of it all.

The home has become the site of incredible moral breakdown in today's world.

Modern society shrugs off divorce as commonplace. Abortions are outnumbering live births in more and more cities.

Children are unstable because they see their parents divided. Marriages decay as each partner trusts the other less and less. *Love* has become a cheap word in Webster's dictionary.

Families are in need today as never before. But that also means the home has great potential for revival.

The modern family could generate the greatest revival this world has ever seen. That's what I'm praying for.

And that's what initiated the concept of a worldwide Prayer Key Family. Maude Aimee and I saw homes disintegrating all around the world, and we pulled our two sons out of the Cathedral's television studios and onto the stage along with our younger son and daughter. Together with our two daughters-in-law and our grandchildren, Maude Aimee and I determined to share with the world our vision for revival in families all over the face of the earth.

We began sharing prayertime together as a family every week on our television programs. We asked families all over the world to join us in prayer for the needs that people had expressed to us by mail.

And we have never wavered from our commitment to the family as God's greatest institution. In every service we hold, no matter where we are on this planet — in the steaming heat of a Liberian summer or the icy chill of a Tokyo winter — our family always gathers around the prayer table to share in prayer.

We have discovered the power of prayer in our own family.

Hundreds and thousands of needs have been met since we established the Prayer Key Family. Lives have been transformed by the power of God. Bodies have been miraculously healed. Broken homes have been mended. Businesses have been rejuvenated as believers have united in prayer and faith.

We have discovered that the principle of seedtime and harvest — a spirit of selflessness, God's law of giving and receiving — is the key to revival in the family today.

I don't encourage people to join the Prayer Key Family because it's *ours*, but rather because I am so excited about *what God can do* when families unite to give of themselves in a spirit of selflessness, obeying God's law of giving and receiving, following the instruction of the apostle Paul:

"Let nothing be done through strife or vainglory; but in lowliness of mind let each esteem (the) other better than themselves" (Philippians 2:3).

14

"It ain't my fault!"

THE LITTLE FOXES

As families strive to live life together and love it down through the years, there are a few practical guidelines that can help.

First, have things in common.

Over and over marriages have failed because one partner subscribes to one religious doctrine and the other partner to another. But the need for a common denominator goes beyond religion or religious forms. It applies to every material possession. Make all of your goods commonly owned, belonging to all members of the household.

As for parents, carry the concept into your relationships with your children. Think of all your children as being yours together. Don't slip into the dangerous syndrome that calls the children exclusively "mom's."

Share activities; share the disciplinary responsibility; share the time and the energy and the love.

Emphasize togetherness. Dad, put God's law of giving and receiving into practice in your house. Give your kids some attention, and you will reap a harvest of peace and happiness in your household. Mom, discipline your children in love, not in anger, and help draw them closer together as brothers and sisters.

Kids, stick by your parents. Don't rely on your buddies for all your entertainment. Parents can still be fun.

And when somebody in your family gets on your nerves, remember to ask yourself the four key questions from Chapter 11 — especially, "Am I giving in order to receive?"

A second guideline for living life in a family and loving it is to . . .

Stay clear of debt.

A young man and woman got married and bought a small home. One day in a department store a salesman told them they could get air conditioning for just a few dollars down and a few dollars a month. All they did was sign for it.

A few days later someone showed them a new refrigerator — for a few dollars down and a few dollars a month. All they did was sign.

Before long they had purchased a new car, a washer and dryer, and a dozen other things on credit.

And suddenly they discovered that their monthly payments amounted to more than their monthly paychecks!

The strain was too much for their young relationship. In a very short time they were in my office for counseling, struggling to avoid divorce.

Finances affect the emotions in a strong and direct way, and it's difficult to round up emotions that have gone haywire over money troubles. Tragically, money problems obstruct hundreds of otherwise healthy relationships every year. "An ounce of prevention," as the old saying goes, "is worth a pound of cure."

Stay out of debt.

Whenever possible, save your money to buy the things you want and pay with cash.

Thirdly, resolve the conflict between "honoring father and mother" and "cleaving unto each other."

Vote for cleaving.

Don't be guilty of allowing your own parents' influence to create conflict between you and your spouse. This is a problem I see over and over in troubled homes.

"Cleaving unto each other" goes further though. It means keeping a positive perspective on your mate.

Years ago I officiated at the marriage of a couple who had very little of this world's goods. They set up housekeeping in a small house trailer. Soon they were bickering.

Then a baby came along. At the peak of frustration, the couple came to my office seeking help.

I had them write down on separate pieces of paper everything that bothered them about each other. Once they saw it all on paper in black and white, they could see that they had really compiled two lists of foolishness.

They had failed to look for the good in each other, and their perspective on marriage had become negative. They were living their lives in reaction to each other, negatively shaping their attitudes and actions and feelings toward each other. They were "cutting off their noses just to spite each other's faces."

Bitterness had crept in. "The little foxes," according to the proverb, "had spoiled the vine."

One of the most pervasive problems in today's families is bitterness.

This is simply the failure to forgive. It is a dangerous failure, however, for it destroys the relationship — it destroys that "cleaving" between husband and wife.

Jesus put a premium on forgiveness.

He included the idea in His model prayer. "And forgive us . . . as we forgive . . . " (Matthew 6:12). In fact, this is the only *requirement* Jesus made of us in His prayer.

Time and again He told stories illustrating the need to forgive. In one parable an unmerciful servant who had already been forgiven a huge debt refused to forgive a tiny debt. He was " . . . delivered to the tormentors" (Matthew 18:34) because of it.

Forgiveness is paramount in God's plan. He bases all of life upon it. Without forgiveness, you and I cannot enter heaven, because we are covered with a sinful nature from the moment of birth.

God forgives us of our sins, and then expects us to follow His model.

Forgiveness fits precisely into the pattern of self-lessness. When you die to self — when you put your own wants on the back burner — you are able to concentrate on the needs of the person who has hurt you. When you ask yourself how you can *give* to that person, how you can *minister* to that person, then forgiveness flows easily.

Forgiveness and selflessness go hand in hand. Both are squarely based on God's law of giving and receiving, and both are essential to living life and loving it.

I've heard people say that they can forgive but never forget.

If Christ said that about our sins, where would we be today? To an extent that may be true. I know a woman whose husband hurt her very badly several years ago. Since then he has asked her forgiveness, and today they have an excellent and cooperative marriage.

She still has not forgotten what her husband did to her, she says today. She remembers it. But she remembers it as a fact in her mind, not as a hurt in her heart. To her thinking, it is history, not biography.

When that wife determined to forgive her husband, she asked the Holy Spirit to heal that hurt she was feeling so deeply. And day by day, week by week, month by month, that hurt eventually vanished. Today, she says, she can't find that old hurt, even if she searches for it.

Forgiveness is an ointment, a lotion, a salve, that cools the burning desire for revenge.

It's necessary for every hurt: large and small, trivial and major. You need to continually forgive every member of your family — for burning the toast, for smashing the car.

Whether the person is right or wrong doesn't matter to God so much as how you handle it in your own heart. It is Christ's spirit to forgive. Take Christ's spirit and learn to forgive.

God, in fact, *commands* us to forgive one another.

"Be ye kind one to another," Ephesians 4:32 says, "tenderhearted, forgiving one another, even as God for Christ's sake hath forgiven you."

God doesn't judge you on the basis of how others treat you, but rather on the basis of how you treat others. *Their* fairness and *their* kindness doesn't even enter into the picture.

You are responsible exclusively for your own heart and soul. I am likewise responsible for mine. It doesn't matter what you think of me, but it makes a difference what I think of you. A man's sinfulness toward me doesn't affect my spirituality at all, until I take it into my own heart and let it shape my thinking negatively. Until then, the other guy has the problem. When I begin looking for revenge, I make his problem mine. I lose, and he wins.

The ultimate question is: What is my relationship with God?

I don't have to answer for you and your relationship with God. I couldn't if I tried. My only responsibility is to forgive you, to love you, and to love God.

Jesus demonstrated this principle in the middle of His agony on the cross. "Father, forgive them" He said of His murderers (Luke 23:34). He looked beyond their sins to their souls.

Take Christ as your example, friend.

When you feel hurt by someone, look beyond the sin and into the soul.

Get soul-oriented. Love souls. Learn to forgive and you will be well on your way to living life and loving it.

15

PURE ANGER

Sure, your anger is going to flare. God created you with a built-in sense of right and wrong.

I spent most of my adolescence in anger.

I despised the conditions my dad had to work in as a country preacher. It made me mad to see him struggling from one meeting to the next, reaching only one church at a time, wearing himself out and barely able to keep his wife and six kids from going hungry.

My only childhood fear was starvation. Would there be a next meal? If so, where would it come from?

It angered me that a man of God like my father had to minister under that kind of burden.

Was the anger justified? Or was it a sin?

From that anger grew a dream to put God on Main Street.

I saw the circus come to town. I watched the rough men chomp their cigars while they hoisted the big-top tent. I watched the huge crowds cram into that tent to see the "world's greatest show."

Even if my parents had allowed us kids to attend something so worldly, they couldn't have afforded the luxury. But I stood outside and clenched my fists — not because I was missing the show, but because of my love for the ministry of the Word of God.

"If God had a tent like that," I muttered through gritted teeth, "He'd have a crowd like that. God ought to be on Main Street."

It was a young teenager's righteous indignation — and a healthy anger. It was focused on a need to reach lost souls with the saving gospel of Jesus Christ. It was the seed of the vision God would give me almost two decades later, when He called me to establish a worldwide television ministry.

What makes you get angry?

Christ got angry at moneychangers dishonoring the Lord God in the temple. The prophets raged and stormed throughout the Old Testament at sinners because they were dishonoring God.

Anger is justified when it springs from pure motivation.

When your anger is purely motivated, it will cause growth in

your spiritual character. Anger that springs from impure motivation will rot you spiritually.

Most anger is the result of feeling abused or shamed. When your preschooler screams through breakfast and throws his food on the floor, you begin to feel taken advantage of. Anger boils up.

But what is your motivation? Is it to teach the child better table manners, or to get your own way with him for the moment?

When you become angry, investigate your motivation before acting on your anger.

Then ask yourself that all-important question: "How can I follow God's law of giving and receiving, and minister to the person or situation causing me to feel angry?"

Anger, bitterness, depression — they all come from the same locker. They are all finally resolved by one method: God's law of giving and receiving.

God's way is truly the greatest method for living life and loving it!

16

NO ONE HERE
WEARS SHOES

Sometimes you feel like a failure. Sometimes you just slump down and say, "Why can't I be like the great people of the Bible?"

But look at Noah. He was a failure. He preached the same message for 120 years and didn't win a single convert outside his own family.

But he did what God asked him to do. *And God blessed him for his faithfulness.*

Look at Peter. He was a failure. He talked big about supporting Jesus in the public campaign, but at the bitter end he denied even knowing Him.

Still, God used Peter as one of the major voices of the early church. *He blessed him for his faithfulness.*

Look at Paul. He was a failure. He spent the first half of his life murdering Christians.

And yet God called him out to be the greatest missionary in history. He was the author of half the New

Testament. *And God blessed him for his faithfulness.*

Our models in the Bible were as human as you and me. They had to find the purpose in their problems, just as we do.

They had to grow through the valleys, like you and me.

But what distinguished each of them was *their faithfulness to God's call*. When God spoke, they acted; and they stuck to their vision. They held on, their whole lives, to that vision. They never let go of that vision.

It can be hard at times.

I know firsthand about holding on after more than a quarter-century of hanging onto the vision God gave me for a worldwide television ministry. It hasn't been easy to stay steady all the time. It has been tempting to grow weary, or depressed, or angry. And at times it has been easy to feel guilty for not being able to do more than I have for the Lord.

"Now faith is the substance of things hoped for, the evidence of things not seen" (Hebrews 11:1).

The story of my own life and ministry is not over because of my "faith in things hoped for, and things not seen." I still have faith that our ministry will be able to fulfill the Great Commission and go into all the world to preach the gospel.

And the story of *your* life and ministry can continue to grow too, as you fix your faith in Jesus Christ and "things hoped for, things not seen," . . . greater and greater things down the road — a forgiving spirit, a prayerful attitude, a faithful lifestyle.

That's how I'm praying for you as I write this book.

I pray that as you apply the principles of Scripture to your everyday life, you'll find yourself living life and loving it more every day.

Take the vision God has given you, and go with it. Be faithful to it. Don't pass it off on someone else, and don't try to take another person's vision as your own. Be faithful to your own vision.

A Methodist preacher from West Virginia drove up to the Cathedral in an old jeep one Saturday. He walked up and down the aisles, wringing his hands and weeping.

"Rex, I pastor five little mountain churches," he said through his tears. "Together, they don't pay me enough to stay alive, so I dig a little coal during the week to sell door-to-door."

He gazed up at the big lighted cross suspended from the Cathedral's domed ceiling and began crying harder.

"Oh, but I wish I could stand proud in God's presence and say I built something this beautiful to the glory of God like Rex did."

"Wait a minute," I said to him. "God called me to this ministry. He didn't call you to do this. He called *you* to those five little churches back in West Virginia.

"If *I* tried to pastor those five churches, I'd probably fail because that's not the vision God gave me. God gave that vision to you. And if *you* tried to build the

111

Cathedral, *you'd* probably fail — because that's not the vision God gave to you."

The preacher blinked and looked at me silently.

"You've got your vision," I told him with a smile. "It's just as God-given as mine. Be faithful to it. Stick with it."

The man's face broke into a wide grin. "I never thought of my ministry that way," he said.

"But I'm going to do it, Rex! I'm going back to West Virginia rejoicing, and I'm going to be faithful to the vision God has given me!"

Wherever you are, friend, God has given you a vision.

He has established a plan for your life. Be faithful to it. Stick with it.

You may find yourself in a shop, in an office, or in the home. *God has placed you there.* Be faithful to Him through that job.

You may not preach to huge crowds, but you can minister right where you are.

Remember that no matter where you are, you are working for God. Your employer simply has the privilege of giving you your paycheck!

I urge you to be filled with the Spirit. That phrase has taken on so many different meanings these days, but in its simplest form it means to become more *God*-conscious than *things*-conscious.

When you first learn to drive, you have to think through every single move you make. You have to concentrate to put your foot on the brake pedal, or turn on the headlights. But as you drive more and more you become less conscious of those activities. They happen almost automatically.

Being filled with the Spirit works the same way. It helps you do *more automatically* the things you have to think hard about in the spiritual realm right now. The Spirit enables you to respond more automatically to others, and to yourself, when you feel tempted or confused or depressed or angry — the way Jesus would respond under the same circumstances.

Remember that your working for God is one part of being God-conscious.

Discovering the power of prayer will also help you to become more God-conscious.

Growing a good crop of faith also helps.

So does developing a forgiving spirit.

Also practicing the principle of seedtime and harvest deliberately in every area of your life.

Everything that makes you more God-conscious, less things-conscious, fills you with the Holy Spirit.

"Seek ye first the kingdom of God," (Matthew 6:33) the Bible says.

Get more God-conscious than things-conscious and God will pour out His blessings on you.

Still, you will surely find yourself meeting the devil along life's way. You will probably meet him all too often to suit you.

I remember one time when my dad was preaching

113

about confronting the devil in such situations. And an old man stood up in the crowd, shook his head, and shouted, "Aw, preacher, you talk about trouble with the devil, but I've been in this church 40 years, and I ain't never yet met the devil once!"

My father replied with a smile, "Of course not! You can't meet somebody if you're walking the same direction!"

Problems are bound to come your way, no matter how spiritual you are, no matter how faithfully you practice the principles of Scripture in your life. The devil will try to trip you up over and over.

We Christians are living in a foreign land, a land that Adam sub-leased to the devil thousands of years ago. The systems of the world are backed by the ungodly. The world does not walk as we do. The world does not think as we do. They do not speak our language nor serve our Lord.

We are seeking a "city . . . whose builder and maker is God" (Hebrews 11:10). We are seeking a Saviour, a Healer, who is perfect and without sin.

He was unsuccessful on earth in the natural sense, in many ways, just like you and me. He was scorned and criticized, ridiculed, hunted, and assassinated. And even though we may face troubles, not even half of the persecution inflicted upon Christ is ever likely to happen to you and me.

Look at your hands. They have no nail-prints. So we are getting off lighter than our leader. Our suffering will never be as great as Christ's, because God is faithful to His own.

In turn, we must be faithful to what God has given us.

Be faithful to the vision God has given you. Stick it out.

God will honor your faithfulness in spite of your shortcomings, just as He honored Paul and Peter and Noah and scores of others.

The world needs faithful men and women of God as never before.

With the earth in growing turmoil, we may be inclined to shut ourselves indoors and keep clear of the ugliness. But God has called us to step out with His truth.

A shoe company in Nashville, Tennessee, sent two of its top salesmen to an area of Africa to analyze its potential as a new market for shoes.

The two men stepped off the plane and their eyes grew wide with disbelief. Every person in sight was barefoot!

One of the men cabled back to America: "No one here wears shoes. No chance for a new market. Coming home."

But the other man cabled, "No one here wears shoes. Great opportunity! Double my first order!"

Our opportunity, friend, is sensational. God has given us the tools to touch the entire world for Jesus Christ. He has given us mass media, instant communications, fast transportation.

All we need to add is the faithfulness.

"Lift up your eyes," Jesus says today, "and look on the fields; for they are white already to harvest" (John 4:35).

"And he that reapeth receiveth wages, and gathereth fruit unto life eternal" (John 4:36).

I'm praying for you right now, friend, that you will be faithful to God, that you will stick with your vision, growing a good crop of faith, living your life for Jesus Christ, and above all, loving it.

And I believe in my heart, upon the authority of His Word, that God will bless you richly and abundantly.

To live life and love it, let us walk in obedience . . .

to man's laws . . .

nature's laws . . .

God's laws.

17

Can you break a toothpick?
Can you stop a seed from growing?
Yes, you can if you want to!

WHAT IS THE
PRAYER KEY FAMILY?

A nyone can break a toothpick, but if you put enough toothpicks together they will become a log. A log so powerful and so strong that no human on earth could break it. Why? Because the Bible tells us there is power in unity: "Two are better than one; because they have a good reward for their labor. For if they fall, the one will lift up his neighbor" (Ecclesiastes 4:9, 10).

Now that you've entered in to the family of God through the Rex Humbard Ministry and this book, you are seeking closer fellowship with Him and other Christians. You feel a desire to share yourself with others, by sharing your needs so others can join in supporting you with prayer, and by sharing of the riches God has given to you.

That's one of the reasons why, years ago, the Lord led me to begin the Prayer Key Family . . . to give strength and fellowship to my friends and partners!

Through the fellowship of the Prayer Key Family, we share one another's burdens in prayer . . . and share the joy of victory as we see our every need turned into miracles.

Through the ministry of the Prayer Key Family, you'll discover a closer walk with the Lord . . . and grow in your faith, knowing your prayers are answered, whatever the need; spiritual, physical or financial!

Yes, there is strength and power in the unity of the Prayer Key Family!

The second reason I felt led to begin the Prayer Key Family was to allow God's people to practice the principle of "seed time and harvesttime" in their lives. "While the earth remaineth, seedtime and harvest, and cold and heat, and summer and winter, and day and night shall not cease" (Genesis 8:22).

Look carefully at a watermelon seed. Through these seeds, God shows us that He lives. God guarantees us that if we sow these seeds, water them and keep the weeds away, each seed will grow a vine that will produce four or five other watermelons.

And within each watermelon there are more than 400 seeds. So each seed, planted, reproduces itself 2,400 times. This is God's way. If we sow the seeds, God will make them grow. What we put into the hands of God by faith is what God will multiply back to us! "Give and it shall be given unto you; good measure, pressed down, and shaken together, and running over, shall men give into your bosom. For with the same measure that ye mete withal it shall be measured to you again" (Luke 6:38).

Throughout the Bible, God always keeps His promises to those of us who plant seeds of faith and expect to reap a harvest of blessings.

As a member of the Prayer Key Family . . . you can know peace, joy and contentment in every trial as well as every victory . . . just as God has promised in His Holy Word. And you'll discover an enriched and fuller walk with the Lord through prayer, study and fellowship!

You will also have the unique opportunity monthly to plant a financial seed of faith into a worldwide ministry that is touching people's lives with the Gospel of Jesus Christ on every continent.

Through our ministry, people by the thousands are being saved throughout the world. They are being healed, blessed and delivered. People are receiving financial blessings like the Bible promises in Philippians 4:19. They are getting jobs, better jobs, raises in pay. They are getting better homes, new cars. Why? Because they are faithfully planting seeds of faith in this worldwide ministry.

Will you put God first in your giving according to Matthew 6:33?

Don't leave God out. Put Him first. Take God as your financial blessings partner.

Without your financial seed-sowing in this ministry, Satan can break its financial back just as easily as you can snap a single toothpick.

And God spoke to my heart that if you hold those seeds back they will not grow. God will have nothing at all to multiply back to you, the sower. This is the only way a harvest of blessings can come back to you. You sow first, then God had something to multiply back in your life.

Right now, you might be saying, "Rex, how can I

become a member of the Prayer Key Family, sow my seeds of faith, and reap the blessings that God has for me . . . and be a blessing to others in this soul-winning ministry?"

There are two things I would ask you to do:

1. Open your Bible to Galatians 6:7: "For whatsoever a man soweth, that shall he also reap." Then I want you to think of your greatest need that you are facing. Sit down and write these needs to me in a letter. It doesn't need to be fancy or even typed. Just write down whatever needs you are facing.

Then, in your heart say, "Lord, I am going to sow a seed of faith in Rex Humbard's ministry that he has maintained for more than 60 years. I am sowing it to help Rex and the Prayer Key Family win lost souls around the world. Lord, as I send you my needs, and my seed of faith, I want Your Harvest blessings returned in my life. I am going to include You in my giving and I want You as my financial Partner. Amen."

Pray this prayer from your heart, and then return to me your needs and your seed of faith gift.

2. In Jesus' name, I am asking you to write to me personally at the address in the front of this book. Let me know that you are committing yourself to be a partner with me in the Prayer Key Family, by planting your "seed of faith" gift in this ministry.

Many may be able to give $15 each month, but at least give a monthly "seed of faith" gift to the Prayer Key Family outreach ministry.

When you do these two things, I will be eternally grateful!

As a Prayer Key Family member, you will receive a beautiful new Prayer Key for your key ring — not just an ordinary key, but a point of contact for you.

Each time you reach for your keys, you'll see your Prayer Key and remember the commitment that we have made to each other — and you'll be strengthened by our common bond of prayer-support for each other.

When you become a Prayer Key Family member, I will also write your name in my new golden Prayer Key Family Book.

Every Wednesday, I will open this book and I will pray for you. I'll ask God to bless you, and to answer your every prayer.

And finally, when you become a member of our worldwide Prayer Key Family, I'm going to send you a faith-building, inspirational letter every month — a letter full of insights from God's Word that will encourage and enlighten you, and help you grow dramatically stronger in your Christian walk day by day.

The Rex Humbard Prayer Key Family is reaching out in love and prayer as never before to one another and also to the world around us.

Become a member of the all new Rex Humbard Prayer Key Family today! And together let's watch the difference this is going to make in the lives of those around us and in our own lives as well.

Now it's up to you.

You've already been blessed through the ministry of this book.

You've taken a serious step, committing your life to the Lord.

Now, you need to put "feet on your faith." You need to step out in faith believing for answers for your needs, and sow in faith by giving.

Send me your prayer needs that you want me to pray over and at the same time let me know you're joining with me in faith and giving — and sow your "seed of faith" gift in the Rex Humbard Prayer Key Family.

Don't forger, what we sow is what we grow. This commitment to the Lord and the Lord's work is the best thing that you have ever done in your life.

Rex Humbard